A LIFETIME

THROUGH LOVE

J. Jeff Cochran

Copyright © 2016 J. Jeff Cochran

All rights reserved.

ISBN: 0692782796
ISBN-13: 978-0692782798

Author's note

I started writing poetry in junior high school as a part of creative writing class and continued ever since. There are over 300 poems of which the majority are included in this volume.

This is my personal journey through love, relationships, marriages, and depression over 50 years. While I am publishing this primarily for friends and family who requested it, I hope other readers will find my words of value also.

My poems are snapshots of feelings through the waves of my life--sometimes rolling gently against the sand of a beach and other times crashing loudly into a rocky shore.

For all those women who touched my heart, I am forever grateful.

We've caught a fading, falling star.
Up we've come, and down so far.
so many word, so many years,
the gentle kisses and burning tears
the glowing fire's brilliant glow
so warm inside when cold winds blow,
the thoughts and joys, so much we've learned,
but while we grew, the tables turned.
The day approaches, streaking fast –
a new day comes to meet the last.
One last path that we build now
to test a trusting, loving vow
a vow to build our lives as one
til love o'er pain is finally won,
when faith and hope and love remain.
the joy of loving, like falling rain.

If I cast your name to the wind,
    I know it would carry a reply.
If I reached my hands far enough to the stars,
    I know I'd feel your fingers in the night.
If I grew cold and still in time,
    I know you're warmth would bring new life.
And if I knew,
    I know you'd know too.
If I played every card right,
    I know you'd play better.
But if I didn't win,
    I know you wouldn't let me lose.
For if I lost that hope,
    ...I wouldn't know at all.

My ship is sailing over the seas
        and flying with the wind
                the waves alone know where she leads
                      and where her course has been.

Her voyages have scarcely touched
        the treasures of her hold,
                for every trade she ventures forth
                      turns her still and cold.

Her sails are strong and silken cloth,
        and sturdy and proud her hull,
                but the clapping of the mighty seas
                      has turned her features dull.

The crew stands able as the best;
        the captain is Supreme.
                But the ship sails on without a home,
                      just floating in a dream.

My ship may meet its fate someday
        or reach a port at last.
                She lives until Hope's flag, that flies,
                      drops slowly to half-mast.

You ask, what good

what good are healing hands to the dying
what good is a soft warm shoulder when hope fades
what good are the tears that streak a young man's face
      when he learns his father is dead
what good is a handshake, a kind word
what good is wishing happiness and love to someone
      who isn't interested
what good is a warm family
what good is caring

What good, you ask
what good then is the sunshine
      and what good lies in knowing
           if you can't feel it already.

I remember, long ago,
    the hazel hair,
    the eyes aglow
      The wind that kissed
        a smile
          and then
            followed one home.
Early times then,
    childhood's games,
      as we tried to win
        to catch and tame
          our songs and hopes
        so innocent
          as we played well.
Roaming free, flying high
    noisy yells
    whispered sigh
    toiling not over war
      and peace
        beauty in our frolic.
We rode through hills
    and valleys low
    where trees do bow
      and grasses blow
    Sharing in our ways
      a joy
      and warmth
        of childhood's dreams.
Then came those days
    our fates were tossed
      diverged our ways
      our paths were split,
    The scene was changed
      and brought
        new friends
      toward childhood's end.
The scene is changed again.
    The wheel of life
      another spin
      those happy days of

                        youth
                        and love
                  now merge our lives anew.
Still those laughs
            and silly joys
            Still the play
                  but newer toys
            Once a care now
                  fulfilled
                  and grown
            Once upon a time.
Later now, past the game
                  we reach out to
                        catch and tame
            new songs and hopes
                  so deep in love
            as we play again well.
I remember, long ago,
            the hazel hair,
            the eyes aglow
            The wind that kissed
                  a smile
                        and then
                              followed one home.

The silent rain, drops steadily on,
lonely thoughts because I'm gone.
There's just the hope as the water flows,
that I'll be home as next wind blows.

There are times that lovers part.
to miss the fondness of heart.
There are times to hope and ache and yearn
all the time 'til I return.

There's a girl I love, , I miss
with her soft light hair and burning kiss.
A girl who's absence makes me blue
that single girl, my love, is you.

God bless and keep you safe for me
until your smile again I see.
My love for you is all I know;
It keeps me warm where'er I go.

I feel the cooling shades of night.
the shadows crawl and cloud my sight.
twilight comes to start nights reign.
and I, to stand alone again.

Remembering as evening now
sows stars as if the sky to plow,
the love we shared anew each day,
the wind and trees that watched us play,

the grass that kissed our wandering feet,
the clouds that hid the sunshine's beat,
the brooks that jelled our growing love,
the joy below the prayers above,

the thunderstorms that caused you fear,
the pounding surf that brought you near,
the warm embrace, the teasing kiss,
the peace of loving that now I miss.

Darkness now has filled the land;
shadows hold my empty hand.
dreams of things that could have been,
and I, to stand alone again.

I remember that first day I saw
    I looked
        searched even,
in many different dreams
    and down various
        avenues and paths.

I looked from the hill
    and with the grasses rolled
        gently down the slopes
            into the verdant valley.

I gazed at the endless
    white caps and pulsating waves
        and tumbled
            and spilled with the pounding surf
        and been dragged
           by the undertow.

I remember that first day
    for it was a time
    when I grew tired of looking
        and feeling
when the wind grew cold and bitter
    and trees
        grew still and cruel
when everywhere I looked
    death oozed
        and darkness conquered.

I stagger through the midst of the storm
        its torrents staying my feet.
        fury drives me from my path.
I move on through the darkness
        I move on for her name rides
            on the wind.
        her spirit guides my steps.

As a lonely ship I lift my bow
        to the smashing waves
            fighting the sea of life
        to reach that shores that must be
            close
                and safe
The great waters stray my course
        as I slip ahead...

But she,
        she floats as my hull
            catches the wind with my sails
            as her spirit leads...
                onward.
        Golden sands reach out
            to greet me,
            the sky comes down
                to cover my face.

you meet me...

and I play my cards by moving
with you and being played with
and you get to know me
but as you get to know me
I get under your confidence
and get to know you
but most of all to understand you.
but then you know I love you
but you resent me for letting you know,
the challenge is gone you say.

I put up with you
and you learn how to accept other people
how to be happy with them
how to love them
and you resent me for this new freedom and life
but you come to love me, need me...
and this you resent most of all

and then you get to know me,
what I go through,
what I feel and how I tick
and then you say I'm too deep, too stuck on self-pity,
too confused, too immature, too bad.
and then its different.
you still need and love me
but not for me
but what I can do for you,
the way I care,
the way I respond to a call
the way I love, the warmth I sow.

but my life inside is alien to you,
as alien as swaying trees are to a polar bear,
but to you, I stay the same
understanding, loving
and it drives deep bitter resentment
and cold and hardness,

but you didn't see it,
you are but another blind soul
seeking the warmth of my light,
but never able to fully look into the light or see it.
don't you ever wonder what keeps that light burning
or how long it will last?

I watch her walk,
        stepping with liquid ease
                gliding over the ground there
        Her sway is as the ocean
                breaking on the shore of my mind
                      with each new wave
                              each new move

Her hips drift up
        then down
                as a ship tossed gently
                      in a calm breeze
The wind caresses her arms
        as they swing, and sweep
                carelessly in the air
        sliding by
                her thighs
                      in time.

Her glowing hair flows
        rolling over her firm shoulders
                like dolphins riding the bow
        her feet fly over
                the seeing carpet of grass
        and she
                is gone forever from sight

But her footsteps linger on.

The fatal surf rolls in again
in superficial beauty,
the lovely snore of wind-shaped dreams
is swept into the sea.
Now many thoughts have crossed this mind
and many words do tell
of the fruitless toil man has in life
and dreams that never jell.
All the hopes I've had are gone,
swallowed by the tide,
and all the love I'd thought was real
has passed me on the side .
But girl I leave you with this wish
that you may find your goal;
Never let the fangs and the life
penetrate your soul.
For I come and go as dawn and dusk
and ride on the wings of breeze.
The minds and hearts of those I've loved
have brought me much I please.
So go your way and search your days
for happiness and peace,
but never let pain hurt your soul
or let your hope to cease.
Someday if warming currents flow,
we may intertwine anew;
then God will save us from the depths
and bring my soul to you.
As the waves surge back and forth
the surf, its strength to show,
no sea could take the faith or love
you've brought my soul to know.

To her the world is a new-found toy,
      an inspiration and interest,
           a path to truth.
To her it is a life-giving flower
      blooming in endless ways-
           a gift of joy.
To her it is a free frontier,
      a place of adventure and knowledge,
           a new capture.
To her it is a goal that must be sought,
      a hurdle to be jumped,
           the challenge of life's tournament.
To her it is an oversized ball of string
      unraveling in every way:
           new hidden secrets.
To her the world is a new dawn;
      a new hope and enthusiasm;
           a new faith.
To her it is the vastness of the sky,
      to catch a falling, fading star-
           one-handed catch.

The radiant beams of dawn's first light
        can steer my path on land
The surging waves of oncoming tide
        can carve my path in sand
The winter storm that floats snowflakes
        can cover deep the ground
The silence round the mountain lakes
        can awe one with no sound
But the paths of men are carved through time
        They follow love in vain
And many men fall from the climb
        broken and torn with pain
Who knows what dreams awaited then
        if the path had been more true
Who knows what life, if and when
        we'd shared real love as two.

The raging seas that toss my fate
and freeze my light so cold,
could never touch my love for you
or make our bonds grow old.
With all the storms and furious gales
my ship is heaved and swamped,
but to your mast stand I rock firm;
The fire for you is undamped.
More than once life's cruise has calmed
while love's sad game was played,
the warmth so strong like Sirens' song
by morn is weak and frayed.
Then one bright star guides home at last
and ends life's search and sail .
It's when the love you've found is true,
when joy and hope don't fail.

Her eyes can touch
      the way I feel
Her words transform
      the way I hear
Her way can turn
      the way I steer
Her mood can form
      my atmosphere
Her tears can cause
      my heart to stay
Her kiss can teach
      my soul delay.

The rustling grasses sweep
    my feet
    stepping with
        padded footfalls lost
            in the symphony of the wind.

The flowing hair breezes past;
    its gold-brown sheen
        softened by
            warming sunlight.

The cooling kiss covers my face
    in secret, silent peace
        and
        soul-sought
            joy.

The trees bow and sway
    in harmonious accord.

In these few quiet moments
        that memories create,
    recapturing dreams and
        old feelings of late,
    Though pockets of details
        are smeared over years;
    the joy and the love
        still live in the tears.
Old fires may smolder
        and blossom to flame
    but players are older
        and wiser the game.
    So lost though I am
        in thoughts of my youth,
    I see through the mist
        the pieces of truth.
We met and we loved,
        we entered one life,
    for a few precious moments,
        husband and wife.

I start this journey wondering
      where my feet will fall
      where my fate will carry me
      where I'll catch my call

Where the lighted paths will be
      and where my soul will flow
      where the joy of love will touch
      where I'll turn to go

Yes, I start this journey wondering
      just what I'm heading for
      just where life's paths will lead me
      and cause my heart to soar.

I, the Poet, stand watching
  you
    on the surf-crested shore
  in the gold-flaked sand
    sprinkled and drifting
      over the beach
        at dawn

I watch the life-warm sun
    rise and spread
  its joy over your tan face
    reflecting
      its light in
        the mirror of your
          sky-color eyes
       and seeming
          smile

I watch as the wind plays
    tricks with your hair
  and spreads
    its carpet over your
      rolling
        shoulders,
     As you stand
       there
         bucking the current
     and repeatedly
       stopping
         the ageless waves

I, the Poet, stand
  watching and
    wondering,
  waiting for the capture...

What shapely bows you slowly bend
        to whisper soft and catch the wind
                amongst your leaves
To take such shape and blossom out
        from rain-streaked trunk so strong and stout
                against the sky
To air your beauty o'er and o'er
        to see the flight of birds that soar
                and hear their song
To cast your shadow with such grace
        that lovers find your limbs solace
                against their world
What warmth you sow in all who gaze
        upon your branches in the days
                when life is green.

Forum at Penn State

The paths of many who strolled before
have streaked this ancient earthen floor,
and pushed their souls to goals unknown,
wandering forth in faith alone.

Seeking through these trails a way
to reach the sky, to touch the day,
to know the secrets old trees share,
to know the world, to know, and care.

And now I stand and ponder too
the same lost secrets they once knew,
I stroll the paths now wide and grown
wandering forth in faith alone.

I am a cloud that carves the sky.
        I know the winds that blow so high.
I feel the warmth the sun burns through.
        I'm free and glad..
                but deeply blue.

I see your fate get tossed and blown.
        I see you quit and watch you roam.
I sense your pain and joy and care.
        And I long all day...
                that I could share.

For easy days are smooth and flow
        with no rough edges or gales that blow.
But you know challenges, and you can learn,
        while I must drift and loaf...
                and yearn.

Margie, your song calls me
        to the dawn
                dawn of love
      promise spread by the
            words of rustling
                    through the grasses
                tipping the trees
                    brushing the golden
                          streaks in your bangs
                                swirling,
                                      falling
                    covering my eyes
                        with their kiss
                  smiling through living
                        strands of sunlight
    Your eyes teach mine
        with the freshness
            and beauty of
                new-fallen snow
        covering my mind with
            a soft, calm blanket
                of joy.
I ride the breezes
    that slide their fingers through
        the luscious forest
            of your hair
                and caress your face
  If I could but
      kiss that smile
          or touch that soul
      riding high
      on the crest of a wave
          that breaks so gently
          that carves so
              beautiful a path
              in the sands of my beach...
Your song calls me
    to the daybreak
        of the sunshine
            that never ends.

Come here fallen angel
        as you once did before,
    when your soul
        was cold and
  barren.
When love's first arrow
      had struck too true,
        And,
            too singularly.
  When pain was a
      non-expressive word.
That time when a smile
      in my eyes began to
ease
    and undertook to light
      a torch
    to be carried against
      such wind.
That time when through
  the mist that clouded
    your eyes
      and mind
  with no dawn to burn it away.
A time I drove
  Apollo's chariot into
    your life
      and opened
    a window,
      a door
    that let brilliant,
      dazzling,
        warming,
          sunlight
    flood your hidden
      troubled soul
And made your thoughts
    trickle
      like a Spring brook
        among the songs
          of birds
            and new grass smells

                                        and cool forest shade
                            growing at both banks
                                    and deepening until
                                        it reached
                                                the delta of your heart.
        That time when
                    you needed
                            ...love.
And now your stream
            freezes over
                            and the door
                                    and window
                                            close,
                            the song
                                    drifting over the hills
                    of the past
                            echoing
                                        a little less
                                                    each time
                                        it recurs.
For now you know the other side
        and love's aim
                has again been too true
                        and
                                too singular
            but this time it isn't you.
    Your revenge
            brought
                    a raging storm
                            to overpower
                                    to hurt.
    Your cruelty
            brought
                    no love
            and the old pain
                    is born again
                                and swirling,
                                        churning,
                                your beautiful
                                        verdant garden-
                                            of your soul-
                                            cold

                                        and barren.
   Come here fallen angel
            as you once did before
                  that time
                        when
                              you needed
                                    ....love.

Stands a girl
           hair gently caressing the breeze,
    twisting and floating over rolling shoulders,
    kissing the gold of a smiling face,
    and slipping over breast with ease.

Stands a girl
           head arched to meet the warm sun,
    swaying and laughing, arms stretched out high,
    soaking in life and giving off beauty,
    beauty unmatched, never outshone.

Stands a girl
           turning slowly and sweeping eyes,
    a whisper of profound silence and secrets new,
    knowing the joy, and careless as wind
    soaring high as any bird that flies.

Stands a girl
           now gazing upon and searching anew
    the paths before, and the trails behind,
    illuminating caches and crevices.
    radiating the light of a chosen few.

Looking from the windowsill
I see the gentle snowflakes spill
The blanket white dusts over the plain
The cold soft beauty of frozen rain,
reaching through the glass

Inside is burning warmth and light,
a shelter from the chill frostbite,
a time of grace and deepest thought,
a time for friendship to be caught,
watching the snowfall

Darkened clouds shroud, once blue,
the sky, now gray and covered too,
Reach not inside and dim my soul.
This peace and brotherhood extol
through all the storms

Looking from the windowsill,
the snow still falls, the flakes still spill.
Blankets white still coat the plain,
with frosty drifts of frozen rain
reaching through the glass

Bookcase

row on row
and stacked away
stamped and numbered
more each day
black and blue
and red and green
large and small
and in between
some are short
some are thick
some are slow
others quick
used are some
and some decay
some replaced
a newer way
a few will live
from now until
the rest have died
as thousands will
I watch them now
In quiet sleep
shelf on shelf
their places keep
waiting to
be used anew
knowledge in
their words imbue.

You once told me you didn't know
    what love was
        but at the same time
            you could see it.
When I told you love
    was the wind caressing
        your smile
    and tossing your hair, in
        not so many words,
           you saw.
When I told you love was
    caring and understanding
    and not pushing or pulling
    but helping,
        in not so many words,
           you saw.
When I told you love was
    life
      a moment forever
        captured on a sandy shore
           in the face of ageless waves
               beating and pounding,
        in not so many words,
           you saw.
When I told you love was
    a poem
        touching your soul
        and leaving
           a deep beauty
               and hope,
        a love in itself,
        in not so many words,
           you saw.
For if I tried to tell you love was
    objective
    or had rules
    or was true or false
    or real or not
    or good or bad
    or free or caught
        in so many, many words
           you wouldn't see it at all.

You once told me you didn't know
        what love was,
           but at the same time
                    you could see it
                            as few can.

You loved me once in theory, though,
      as if the tide were low.
You love me now in ember light
      where a fire once did glow.
You love me now with roving mind
      and roaming soul as well.
You love me now with different mood
      that used to soar but fell.
You love me now with sympathy
      as if I now am past.
You love me now as if I raced,
      tried hard, but finished last.
You love me now but not in light;
      your heart has flown away.
You loved me once in spirit
      but your spirit's gone astray.

Why again
      this subtle pain,
the joy of loving
      like falling rain?
Why so weak
      to slip again
and try love's game
      but never win.
To try to catch
      a wind so fair,
to ride so high,
      such youthful dare
giving wings
      to beat a storm
that soon will birth
      to darkly form.
Why again to
      leave the shade,
to stray afield
      where safety laid?
To feel the stinger's
      sting anew,
to watch my sky
      turn deeper blue.
Why again
      to feel love's grasp,
the fatal bite
      of a golden asp.
Why to fall
      in love again-
the joy of loving
      like falling rain.

Let me sing of you and I,
      lifted hearts to touch the sky,
faith so deep no ocean's match
      catch the breeze, bare-handed catch.
Running free along the sand,
      sharing sunlight hand in hand,
cooling surf fresh in our ears,
      gentle winds melting fears,
with the tide our rising dreams,
      race our souls to trap sunbeams.
Lifted voices crying high--
      live together, and love, or die.
Let me sing of you and I,
      happy song forever nigh.

I try to match your step,
        that way I'm sure of staying close.
You smell like love,
        that must be so,
               for what I smell is dear to me and new.
An arm-in-arm little stroll through town
        becomes a journey--
               a love vacation from ourselves
                      but with ourselves.
Everything you say is funny or beautiful.

Cry in the night
  and I hear.
Whisper to the falling rain,
  sigh as the wind
    howls against the panes
      and pains
Tears,
  slowly rolling
    down your cheek
    dripping,
     Streaking,
      ever so gently
     and lightly
       the misted window.
Thunder,
  booming forth afar,
    touching so close,
    echoing
     in your emptied soul,
     and rebounding in your mind.
Lightning,
  shattering the rhythm
    of the storm,
     pleading in the night
The raindrops dripping,
  Falling,
    Splashing,
     a tear wets
       My out-stretched hand.

Standing lovely on a hill
All alone and silent still
Longing

Wind kissed hair so deeply brown
Crying eyes and head bent down
Hoping

Eyes so deep reflect a star
Pace so gentle from afar
Praying

Warm hands reaching, turn around
 A nervous smile, but peace is found
 Caring

Soft, deep eyes, so great a lift
All around so great a gift
Loving

I've watched you before,
    your eyes looking up
        gently
            searching and full of
                Hope,
        though confused and lost.

I've watched you before
    years ago at first young,
        sweet, you were tormented
            by silly fears,
        lifted by a child's love flowers,
        smiles, happiness--
        gay but concerned
        for life's simple worries,
            and trials.
                sensitivity
                      of a genuine princess

Yes, I have watched you before.
    love touched you then
        as I
        joy and depth
        a wonder still challenging,
            to be explained,
            Discovered,
        loving not easy,
          but full,
            light and warmth,
                to brighten a gentle face,
                to perk up
                      smiling eyes,
                to ease simple
                    Pains,
                to hold
                  as silent peaceful sleep,
                so beautiful as you lie.

I've watched you before--
    Grown,
    Alive,

```
           now you look up lost,
              confused,
                    a woman to face
                       the daylight in morning,
                       the twilight at night,
                       the ecstasy,
                          and agony of
                             Self,
                          and sureness and security,
                          and happiness and love,
           and I to
           look and really see
                 light,
           reminding me of the years,
                 and in the
                       moments forever,
                             around the turn,
           realization--
                 the silent vigil,
                       the endless watch,
                             is ending.
```

I wander slowly paths unknown
    through forest dense and overgrown
        while grasses grow and reach knee-high
            and soaring birds carve out the sky,
    where morning's light warms the dew
    and twilight turns the sky ink blue,
        where branches bend and drop so low
        as if in dance to and fro.

I wander through the rain of years
    where clouds of raindrops shaped as tears
    drench all life in darkened gloom
    with lightning flash and thunder boom
When autumn sun turns leaves to brown
    and dried out grass takes on a frown
    then raging, swirling winds arise--
        tormented storms then fill the skies.

I wander silent the same old way
    but, lo, the dawn has found this day.
    I hear bird's laughter ringing clear
        and rustling trees are singing near.
Streaming light overcomes the night,
    the warming sunlight beaming bright.
    I wonder if, around the bend,
        I'll capture love and journey's end.

Twas a time I waited,
      years and years ago,
with hand out-stretched to reach you,
      to share a love aglow.
Though barely touching,
      you took that trust and care,
and with the first new breeze,
      you left me holding air.

Again a time came to be
      to offer love anew,
but this time more than hands alone
      were stretched to give to you.
With holding you a little more,
      again you took the call.
and when the next breeze hit you,
      left me there to fall.

The third time now is at hand
      for you to see love true,
and you now finally reached out first,
      as I did twice to you.
And reaching just to stroke your face,
I know I mustn't show
      the tears and pain so deep inside,
as I turn and go.

It seems I've loved you so many years
through Christmas joy and New Year's tears.
In spring, the footprints in the grass;
In Fall the chill that comes too fast,
summer's surf and peaceful night,
seasons all – you've been my light.

It seems I loved you yesterday
Your sweet, soft smile that made my day
memories float across my mind--
the laughter, love, you helped me find,
the silly words, the kiss, the clutch,
the little girl I loved so much.

It seems I couldn't have loved you more
than all these things I loved you for.
It seems absurd to love so deep,
to smile as you beside me sleep.
To love and care a million ways,
a million, million yesterdays.

It seems I love you more each thought,
for in your eyes a star I've caught.
It leads one through the darkest hours,
with bowing trees and fields of flowers,
feeling love soar to that star,
tomorrow will be twice that far.

```
Look before you
        and see
        the tears of the rain
                the embrace of the snow
                        drop by drop
                                flake by flake
        covering
          surrounding
                reaching
                    but
                    as a single candle
                            harboring
                            so silent
                                a warmth
                                    as dry logs
                                        cracking in a fireplace
            A chance
                    your questions
                            your eyes
                    love ,
                            I...
Look before you
```

Ode to a past mistress

To leave an angel still in flight,
to face the darkened,
      cold, still night
           alone.
It seems her light, so softly fair
is sign of love
      so very rare
           and warm.
So deep her eyes are speaking more;
the silent brimming
      at eyelid's edge
           of tears.
It seems so strange to turn and go,
to leave this angel
      I love so
           dearly.
It seems we shared so much so fast,
portraying the hope
      that it would last
           forever.
But there are paths that I must seek
and by another's
      side I'll sleep
           soon.
And as I go I leave this care
that all we had
      you too may share
           again.

Go dear love,
  but don't be sad,
if by chance you should look back,
  you will see that familiar smile.

Sad?
  how could I be sad?
    knowing so much more of love
  than I did before.

Hurt?
  you gave me new eyes to view
    the world
  that is a gift for which
    anyone should be grateful we shared

Love... poems...rain...bliss...love...
  We together
    Laughed...cried...worked...loved...
We had our Camelot
  Lancelot and Guinevere
    laughing
      sharing in the sunlight.

You're going toward a much greater love
  than mine.
and I?
  I will find love again
  now that you have taught me
    how.

Go dear love,
  but don't be sad.

At times I feel I've known her
        each passage in my life,
as if she's always been there,
        my newly wedded wife.
As if the word forever
        was flowing as a stream,
and I was floating gently
        wherever I might dream.
A current with no ending,
        and with an unknown start,
the trickling, splashing laughter
        swirling round my heart.
This brook within my feelings,
        the promise and the past,
runs ahead, both clear and true,
        filled by love to last.

Could I compare you
      to what I had before?
Those lovely hours in my room,
      no knockers at my door.
The taste of beer each weekend,
      the dismal Sunday morn.
Cool nights to go to bed alone,
      just blankets to keep warm.
The thrill of love to dream about,
      but empty arms to hold.
The many dinners far from home
      and many dinners cold.
The solo walks through countryside,
      just whispers in the trees,
the birds so high and far away,
      their songs lost in the breeze.
Could I compare you
      to what I had before?
The emptiness around me,
      the nothings to explore.
Can one compare an angel,
      soaring into flight,
with anything that flew before
      through darkness into light?
I was lost and lonely
      like an orphaned fawn,
until your love reached out to me
      and brought my life the dawn.

Darkness greets me at the door
               and welcomes my thoughts.
        Lovely eons seep past
              crying tears so dry
                     and still.
If I were a tree,
    branches bare and dark,
        I could whisper
      to the winds in quiet echoes
          and silent screams
               as they shivered their way
                    through my limbs
If I were a road
    I would be much-travelled
        and well-known
    but seldom used recently
          overgrown, untended,
            dry and lumpy,
                ancient paths still carved
                    in my soil
If I were the sea
        like the night around me
    I could swell
    and wave
        and cover all things
           washed ashore
               on smooth toned rocks
                  and warm sandy,
                      sunlight
beaches
        and I could rise
          and fall, rise and fall,
              rise and fall ever so gently
                and calmly
                    drifting. . .
Have I been seen,
    or felt,
        and known before?
If I were a place,
    could I be found,
        myself.

I wonder could you be more loved
      than in the sunlit Spring,
with sunrise creeping up to you
      and sparking you to sing.
When sunbeams wander through your hair
      and lighten its soft strands,
leaving traces in your smile
      and gentle, soothing hands.
I can speak but to your eyes,
      that melt me in a glance.
Teach my soul to seek what warmth
      and with it love to chance.
For all my words are never enough
      and all my looks can't say
how beautifully and preciously,
      you're loved this springtime day.

When promises came, I was young
        and happy,
                eager of love and freedom,
struck with wonder and joy,
            and gentleness,
            and you.
Promises made me older,
            and unhappy,
        spirit worn and heavy.
Struck without you,
            only promises
                  remain.

Daybreak cracks the still of night;
The yet dark room now streaked with light.
The chill of morn seeps through warm,
and wakens softly, life reborn.

From depths of sleep to sense anew
morning's splendor covered o'er with dew.
The living glow that fills the skies
and lights the dream besides me lies.

The streaks so gentle on her cheek
wiill soon accomplish what they seek.
And she, a dawn, will blossom fair
in love, so deep, that harbors there.

Before she turns from gentle sleep
and floods my day with beauty deep,
capture, I, fair mornings dove.
Can she know how deep my love?

Let's look at love
                Again...
    Let's see it like we did
                when a summer afternoon
                        was a lifetime, and
                                every smile, a rebirth,
                                        like a baby's sigh.
        Remember when eyes would speak
                for hours in seconds
                    and tears were gentle creeks,
                        sparkling, flowing, washing
                            across the banks of your cheeks
                                to greet me,
                                        lift me to the wind.
    We used to stroll into our dreams
                waltzing, whirling
                    through a sea of starshine
                        and beaches of moondust
                                touching but fingers
                                        and knowing...
    But ever not knowing then
                the island we created,
                        the eye of a hurricane.
    Was it so long ago
        we wrote messages on the mirror?
                As if we reflected too
                    the world's joy
                            as we skipped along in the sun.
            We shared winter fires
                and warmth so deep
                        to fight frost-bitten noses
                                and fingers.
                        Then to slumber, sheltered,
                            like trees limbs
                                dusted by
                                        a new blanket of snow.
    When the rains fell,
        who cared whether we
                ducked under cover
                    or stood getting soaked,

                    seeking a kiss
                as the raindrops
                    streaked or faces and hearts?
Was it so long ago
    We looked at love?

    Love used to look at us

Sonnet

It's we who turn, in times of troubled past,
Our gaze upon the stars, to wishes cast;
Who lament love and try to catch its wind.
Can we know what has struck so true and fast?
That warmed our hearts, so deep but doesn't last.
So onward seek us, through this timeless night,
Another shining beacon to our sight.
Perchance, its radiant joy our fears to mend;
But chance we not to let our hopes delight.
For darkness soon will blanket too, this light.
We watch anew the ancient drifting sky.
And glimpse the stars, our reaching cares would hold.
And bid us bathe in faith of ages old
That we have chanced to love before we die.

Of time I have plenty,
        of thoughts plenty too.
words flow so easy;
        so much still to do.
filled are my hours;
        fast fly the days.
evenings are sleepless,
        quick lost in the haze,
somewhere ahead,
        I sense a soft light,
so warm in the darkness,
        so strange to the night.
and waiting beside it,
        a smile in her eyes,
soft-spoken and gentle,
        my sweet angel lies.

    In spite of myself
        I can see you.
        The rains that cloud
            my soul and hamper love,
      the puddles of thoughts that
        tense to the flash
          of lightning,
            surrounding,
              drowned by the thunder
              and splashed by
                  the wind,
      leave me cold
        and shivering,
          alone in a storm
            that howls and rages
              flooding over sense of life.

    Through newborn eyes
        I can see you
        The tears that fall
           diluted by the storm
              dripping
                streaking
                  the dark puddle
          warm to the cold
            pure of love and
              desperate hope.

    When it snows,
        we'll laugh
            at its gentleness
            together
              and snowflakes etched
                with love
                  will streak your heart
                    where tears one did.
        Only my eyes
            will say enough
              about
                  loving you.

Your smile reminds me
    of a time when sunlight
        was my only love
    when swaying trees
        etched the clouds,
            shattering
                the sky
        with traces of golden light
    blossoming in my soul...
        when
            soft carpets of grass
                lay all around
                    my cares.
Your smile is a Springtime
    of awareness
        a re-awakening
    perhaps
        the freshness has
        been dozing,
            waiting
                for the door you opened.
If I told you I loved you
    so early
        in our morning
    you wouldn't understand.
    nor are simple thoughts
        enough
            to show the dawn,-
    the gift of love
        you've sewn
            in the fields of my heart.
But your smile reminds me
    and the sunlight will follow
        long after
            only shadows remain
                to warm me.

Run to me April
      and kiss me with rain.
Call to the Springtime
      and kiss me again.
Sparkle the sunbeams
      caress me with light
Freshen the blossoms
      and dazzle my sight.
Stir up the breezes
      tossing my hair
Wake up the forests
      as I wander there
Sing to the birds
      that circle the sky
Kiss me, dear April
      and teach me to fly.

It seems when things get really down,
It's nice to have your love around.
When it's dark and cold outside,
It's nice to have our souls collide.
When woes and worries of today
find emotions on which to play,
It's your touch that pulls me through-
a gentle smile that makes you you.
In all my years of married life
through happiness and trouble strife,
It's nice to know that you're the one
who lies beside me each new sun.
So when we're old and life is slow
with less to do and less to go,
you'll be there to hold my hand,
for you have shown me promised land.

On this day of winter's chill
when outside, all is still
except the wind that softly blows
and beckons on the coming snows.
We'll snuggle close and watch the trees
bending slowly in the breeze.
We'll build a fire burning bright
to keep us warm throughout the night.
On my shoulder you'll dream away;
The love we've found will always stay.

With a lampshade over morning
        or mist to soften day,
your kiss a sweet awaken,
        gentle as we lay,
silent, smiling, loosening
        the dreams in our eyes,
opening love's window shade
        as nighttime slowly dies.

With child you are
another time,
another day,
for nursery rhyme.
And even though
this is our last,
we'll keep the memories
soon to pass.
The day approaches,
though very slow,
when we as three,
will feel the glow
as then as four.
Our family grows;
deep in our hearts,
our love still knows
how great the joy.
Our laughter soared
when three was born
and so adored.
As we love
our number four,
will we think,
just one more?

Technology of Management

Of systems dynamics
        and theories galore,
with myriads of data
        and software to store,
Why always business,
        Education, ignore?

Well, business is money.
        that we all know!
And computers make millions;
        We can't let that go!
So business is high,
        and education is low.

For students cost money,
        and teachers do too.
our computers can save it,
        so we know what to do:
Buy more computers
        so schools have them too.

Then students learn business
        with kids of their own.
There'll be more computers
        than all that we've known,
and all that choice data,
        how much it'll have grown!

So to stem all these ills,
        we'll system a base
to manage the data
        and save one poor race
from crazy Charles Babbage
        and Countess Lovelace.

Alternate National Military Command Center

I spend this time a'wondering
just why the fuck I'm here.
Whatever did possess me
to come this time of year?
And to this site, of all of them,
why did I pick this one?
Even in the daylight hours
it scares away the sun.
It's like the U.S. Army
created hell on earth,
and when they're short of morgue space
they schedule here a birth.
The snow falls here in buckets;
the wind rips through your clothes.
McKinley still is president
as far as anyone knows
Maybe it's in Maryland,
but it could be in PA,
neither wants to claim it,
so it's tucked neatly away   .
in the foothills of oblivion
and the forests of unknown.
No need to ever find it,
so no dials are on the phone.
They say you can take anything
and last for three full days,
but they've never spend the night here
or stumbled through morning's haze.
"All's well, that ends well"
is the motto on the gate,
and when you first pass through the same
you know you're screwed by fate.
But hope, they say, do not despair
for soon you'll be back home.
Just trust before your next return,
they'll spray with EMCO foam.

It seems to me,
        I've heard the snow
speak your name
        so long ago
and call to me
        in winter's white,
that love for us
        might start that night.

And then as snow
        again to fall,
swirling soft
        another call,
to take a wife
        from now until
the winter's wind
        forever's still

The snow brings life,
        a newness soon
from love as two
        a child will bloom.
To bring anon
        a special glow,
then we as three
        We'll greet the snow.

I hear a calling
        so soft afar,
reaching for
        our hearts again.
Listen, love,
        another call,
as snowflakes softly
        start to fall.

What can I tell you?
    We've lost and we've gained.
We've laughed in the sunshine
    and drowned when it rained.
Snowfalls have kissed us
    while cuddled our souls.
Lightning has zapped us
    and left gaping holes.
We swim in an ocean
    tossed by the tide
drifting in currents
    but still side-by-side.
The wind is our friend
    and lifts us up high,
but chill are the breezes
    and coldly we fly
bound to each other
    by some unknown tie.
We're destined to laugh
    then only to cry.
Our paths often cross
    just gently intertwined
like ivy in summer
    through each other's mind.
Who knows in the morning
    what daylight will bring
the tear of a rainfall
    or love's song to sing.
We face tomorrow
    unhitched to the past;
Your eyes to my eyes,
    I know what you ask.
What can I tell you
    that's certain to be?
I know that I'll love you
    as long as we're we.
For touched are we both
    though each in his way.
In love and in marriage
    forever we'll stay.

Ask me when twilight
        creeps up on us two,
for then only then,
          might I know what's true.

You must think it odd
 to see me just stare
 at a blank piece of paper
 and words forming there.

But inside's a wellspring
of thoughts rarely heard
and once in a great while
I must write the word.

For I am a Poet,
I live in a tree,
when touched by the spirit
I gotta be me.

Soon now I'll climb down
and back to the norm
until when the next time
the words start to form.

Can you know me in morning
      like you know me at night,
when soft dawning sunbeams
      bring day to light?
Can you follow my memories
      and thoughts through the day,
while there at my side
      and in mind all the way?
Can you handle deep feelings
      that darkness knows true,
lasting through sorrows
      and skies not so blue?
Can you linger in daylight,
      like evenings so warm,
when passion surrounds us
      and words know no form?
If our lives slowly mingle
      and life becomes we,
when daybreak awakes us
      what will we see?

In this twilight
        reaching out,
I touch the sea
        and whirl about
to face the breeze
        that stiff caress-
that warms the beach
        of loneliness
with the rumbling and
        twirling tide.
The sandy mist
        is on my side.
Turn my thoughts
        shades of you
as daylight slowly
        changes hue.
Walking on
        surrounded so
With life and, love...
        I used to know.

Stop to ponder
      so much more
than sandy surf
      and ocean roar,
crashing waves,
      a niche in time,
to hear anew
      the rhythmic chime,
a soothing touch
      a deepened mood,
of peaceful thoughts
      no cares to brood.
a shore of hope
      from which to sail,
that all who need
      no longer ail.

I remember that, first day I saw.
    I looked,
        searched even,
in many different dreams
    and down various
        avenues and paths.
I looked from the hill,
    the grasses rolling
        gently down the slopes
            onto the verdant valley
I had gazed out over the endless
    whitecaps and pulsating waves,
        tumbling
         spilling
           with the pounding surf
            and dragged
                by its undertow.

I remember that first day,
    for it was a time when
I grew tired of looking
    and feeling,
when the wind grew cold
    and bitter
and trees
    grew still and cruel,
where everywhere I looked
    death raged
        and darkness conquered
            light.

I remember that day
    and dream of the sights
        I'd lost
            by looking
                instead of seeing
for life is not a game
    to be played
    or a gem to be looked at
        like a construction site
           viewed from a passing sidewalk

                    to be seen and enjoyed
                        and paid for
                            but to be passed in a moment
                                having not deep involvement
                                    or analysis
I remember that first day,
        long ago when
                death came
                        with the wind
                    to take your
                        fairness from the world
                            and the light from my eye
                                in one lethal breeze.

There was a time
        when I looked with hope,
        absorbing the waters of life
                and sorting
                        And counting their treasures.
        a time when I knew the faith
                of discovering and looking
                    through the mists
                            for understanding truth
                                and peace of mind,
                that time when I sought
                        immortality of spirit
                            and searched out
                                broadened horizons of knowledge
        when my soul gave love,
                and sought
                            warmth and care
                                    and joy,
        and looked out on life
                with the blindness of time.

I remember the day I first saw
        with the smile
                    your eyes had brought
                            and the carefree light
                                    you shown
                                            on me

Grandmother Birthday

As we gather together,
this bright April day,
I put down some thoughts
and feelings to say.
Our family is scattered
all over the world;
for some of our loved ones
these words won't be heard.
But remembered they must be,
as we meet again,
to celebrate living
through the joy of our kin.
These ties that have bound us
are joyful indeed;
They bring love and faith
where're our lives lead.
Today is most special,
with sunshine and mirth,
as we gather to honor
this great Lady's birth.
Through her we are family,
from love in her heart,
all share the joys
and warmth from her start.
We wish to you health,
and life's full elation,
until we gather next year
for that celebration.

Its quiet now
      peaceful
            but empty without you.
Music fills my ears
      and eyes
            but not my longing.
Night skies have begun
      dark, windy,
            bringing more than chills.
There's always dawn
      I know,
            hope in warmth light.
Missing you is hard
      unhappy
            but worth the wait.

Don't ask me if I love you,
        or ever miss you much,
or how it feels to want you
        and linger from your touch.
Seek my eyes for deepness,
        trickling like a stream;
Kiss my lips for passion;
        stay with me in dream.
Know me in bright sunlight,
        whisper to my ear,
walk with me at evening,
        hasten to stay near.
Laugh with me at life's ways,
        remember all we share,
Treasure each new moment
        in this love we dare.
Keep this growing warmth we feel
        that we may never part.
Don't ask how much I love you,
        just know it in your heart.

<u>For David and Cindy</u>

Six long years have come and passed
and put this love to test.
Six long years to make hopes last
and prove this union blest.
Gather we this summers' day,
our hearts and prayers to soar,
and wish these two along their way
in loving joy forevermore.
Some of us have gone before,
and some will follow on,
to build upon the family core
and bring new life to dawn.
To wed, to share, from now until...'
the lives we celebrate,
that life ahead will grow and fill
the vows we dedicate.
Go, today, with this fond dream
from all of us, now here:
Catch the sunlight's gentle beam
and harvest more each year.
For there are promises to keep
and labors to be done.
Always, may your love be deep
as now, from two, you're one.

I thought you might be wondering,
after all the time that's passed,
if I remember loving you
and if the passions last.
If my thoughts ever turn to you
and if I ever feel sad.,
that time and place got in the way
of sharing warmth we had.
I know mere words can't take the place
of eyes and smiles and laughter,
or ever match the glowing peace
held, together, after...
But, be these words a gentle touch;
a song; a lingering kiss.
That you may know when night draws high,
it's you I dearly miss.

There come to be,
such times as now,
when clouds appear--
I know not how.
When all around
the shadows fall,
and wonder I
if this is all
that life had planned
for me to do,
for dreams to turn
a darker blue.
If there perchance
may come a light,
warm and soothing
to my sight.
To lead me through
these troubled ways,
for happiness
to touch my days.
That when again
these times appear,
a fairer wind
may I to steer.

I miss you and the reasons clear-
you are there and I am here.
It's nothing new to be apart,
to hold you close just in my heart,
to ponder of you in mid-day
when work's ambition fades away,
to search your eyes that in my mind,
another of your smiles I'll find,
to make time's march a sweeter pill
to turn the noises, soft and still.
Gently now it snows anew
the drifting wind brings me to you.
That when, again we laugh and play,
it will save a rainy day.
Perchance, another day like this
when again, your loving's missed,
captured warmly by your charm,
we stroll my thoughts, arm-in-arm.

For the first time in my life
  I lost
    badly.
I played well
  or, at least, played
   The game was new
    the rules
      changing,
        uncontrolled.
I was not a spectator.
Perhaps I should be.
Perhaps
  I am now,
     for the first time
       in my life.

I knew I had to write these words
but know not where to start.
There are such overwhelming songs
yet flowing through my heart.
The times that nearly ended us
loom large this summer day,
fear that tears may fall again
and I may go my way.
So long ago with this same heart,
we made a tarnished vow,
that through the years of tempered love
kept us home somehow.
She came into my life one May,
this girl that troubles you,
and came again some ten years hence
when I was lost and blue.
By August she was gone again,
because I came to see
who you are and where you are
and what you'll always be.
You came first to me at Christmas
with winter's special charm;
I'll never know what prompted you
to laugh and take my arm.
We grew as one and then apart
and then as one anew
and on a summer day like this
we sealed our lives as two.
Then soon we fostered children
and bills, and fights, and pain;
all the love and joy and dreams
were washed away like rain.
I thought that I could leave you
and live a better life--
so lost and hurt I could not know
you only find one wife.
The grief last year has brought new strength
but, oh, how great the toll.
No worse could I have shattered you,
left scars upon you soul.

Tomorrow is not seen today;
you stare so hard for signs
that I again will steal the fruit
and leave you with the rinds.
You give me all the love I need
and keep my life intact.
You fill in all the simple things
that somehow I had lacked.
I am not trapped to be with you
but am your slave and mate.
I'm sorry that it took so long
and almost was too late.
When now I wake in morning light
and you are lying there,
I do not want to leave your side
for we have much to share.
For as the seasons ever change,
whatever we may face,
I have found my greatest love
and in my heart your place.
I am just for you, my angel,
with every breath I take;
forever and for always now
all others I forsake.
You are my life and loving
and in you, every dream.
Whatever storms may come along
will wither into steam.
I make this promise to you,
in all the years ahead,
that you will know and understand
these simple words I've said.
With all my thoughts and feelings,
if nothing else is true,
no greater love has any man
than this I have for you.

When we look back
      from then to now,
upon the day
      we took our vow,
we smile, and laugh,
      perchance, it seems,
our lives have grown
      on simple dreams.
Looking forward
      from now to then,
as we are one
      where two had been,
We smile for you,
      and wish you might
grow forever
      in love's warm light.

I sense in you a twinkle
that was not there before,
a special laughing, haunting
that warms me to the core.
And in your heart a softness,
the touch of love belies
a long and tired sadness
that hides behind your eyes.
A hope that in our moments,
of gentleness and peace,
with love and growing closeness,
your fears will start to cease.
That in your troubled efforts
to stop your own life's storm,
when its cold and raining--
I'm here to keep you warm.

Just yesterday
      along the shore
I asked of life:
      Is there not more?
I watched the ocean's
      breakers smash
the lonely beach's
      dreams to dash.
I could not see
      through love's eyes
beyond the waves
      what truly lies.

Just then today
      with morning's sun,
I knew of life
      I'd just begun.
There you were
      in summer sand,
to touch my heart
      and take my hand.
And with love's eyes
      across the sea,
the only dream
      was you and me.

```
Death flirts with me
        Why?
                the fatal attraction ...
        It happens near me,
                it threatens around the corner
                        and it calls
                                softly
                                        to me, today,
                                                like before.
No fascination, but interest,
        seemingly always so close,
                ready to appear,
                        or strike,
                                or flirt.
Temptation does not grow
                but interest does.
        The grief eases,
                the hope subsides,
                        the opening is there
                                and the courage--
                                        the why? is not.
Is it peaceful ,
        tranquil
                eternal
                        sleep
                                or
                        just the end.
```

On a day like this
        I need you
    alone in a field
      I stand
    there's a chill around me
        and the sunlight is not warm
           where is the wind?
If I move, I go nowhere
      for so large is the space
        around me
           I see forever
              but what do I see?
If I turn around
      it is the same
        there is no direction
           which way is the wind...
              blowing?
I want to lie down
    and melt
    and fall asleep as the snow
        blankets my face
    to become the space,
      the forever,
          the field in sunlight -
not warm
      but so near.
If it weren't for the wind
        I'd fall.

```
To come so near
        in such short time
                and find you still away
for one mistake
        so long ago
                forever I may pay
What made me blind
        to turn and miss
                the beauty in your eyes,
 to touch your heart,
        to know your love ...
                now deep within me, cries?
What one knows now,
        could one have known
                so many years ago?
With just one day
        of laughs and tears,
                we again would grow?
To share your life
        with just our words
                brings my life a star
that let me touch
        your cheek again
                as if you weren't afar.
No greater love
        I've ever felt
                then this within my heart,
with dreams to hold
        that someday find
                us living, not apart.
```

How can I give you
        the joy in my heart?
Through no poet's words
        could ever I start.
I love you, my Linda,
        more than I know,
the wind of my spirit
        forever to blow.
Forever to touch you
        with gentle delight;
Forever to greet you
        in soft mornings' light.
Whatever the morrow
        spins for us two,
I have but one spirit
        and it stays with you.
It comes when you call;
        it listens and hears.
It's followed your life
        for so many years.
Love, to be with you,
        to hold and to care,
to build for our lives
        so much yet to share.
I have not forgotten,
        my angel divine,
the touch of the summer,
        the kiss of white wine.
Still in the forest
        how clearly I see
that whatever both feel
        was just meant to be.
When you awaken
        and first meet the dawn,
when wet is the dew
        on leaves of the lawn,
let the sun warm you
        and brighten each day,
knowing I love you
        each step of the way.

Let me remember,
      love of my days
(angel of beauty
      in so many ways),
the hours of knowing
      you and your love,
the minutes of sharing
      that lift me above
these shadows I suffer
      and hope to endure
through nights all alone
      throughout this next year,
the gentle caresses
      when we are one,
the glow of your face
      when loving is done,
the breeze in your hair,
      the spark in your eye,
the song when you laugh,
      the depth when you cry,
the lines of your figure,
      the curve of your soul,
the love you etched
      on my heart (that you stole),
the devilish smile
      the teasing refrain,
this shelter of love
      from now falling rain.

It's true
    I chose to leave the road
        to take a less traveled path
   There is such spectacle
      quiet, peace,
         solitude
   and now,
      darkness
         so close to the start.
A fork
   whose divergence
      leads
         where? and why?
   Time does not
      seem kind
         on such a long,
           endless path,
             Why so sharp a fork?
A turn
   once made
      irreversible,
         dangerous,
           foreboding
              unknown...
The peace
   unsettles,
      the breeze dies,
         it is cold
a chill in summer
   death hangs on the tree limbs
      time stops,
         waits
Each way,
   has thorns and berries,
      I bleed and savor
         already.
But is there
   a choice
   a truth?
How long ago
   did I leave the road?

Touch my shadow
      that you may know
           me
Bring me the soft
      gentle breeze
           in your hair
Caress me
      with the song
           of your words
Teach me
      with your eyes
Drive the dark
      away

There is a path
      I once knew
           less overgrown
                wider
                      but no less beautiful
I've lost the way
      it wanders
           meanders
                slopes
                    but doesn't end
                        and cannot lead

Deep ahead
      it knows
           no end, no beginning
I used to know
      the trails
           and trees
Where are you in
      the dark?

You used to
      know me

No words I write
      are quite the same
as thoughts that bring
      to mind your name,
of things you say
      with just a glance,
of love we seek
      and dare to chance,
the years of longing
      behind each kiss,
the time together
      we dearly miss,
the greater joys
      that yet must be
beyond short minutes
      that we now see.
If it were mine
      I'd change the wind,
with gentle breeze
      these words I'd send:
"Come and linger
      so warm and near",
soft we'd lay
      with naught a fear,
to have and hold
      all through each night,
to laugh forever
      in morning's light,
To stroke your cheek
      and slowly find
you nestled snug
      within my mind".
But even if
      the wind won't move,
I'm thankful for
      the times that soothe,
For tender smiles
      we share as two
that turn my fancy
      back to you.

Caress my soul
        and touch my heart
that to you, love,
        I may impart
the depth of joy
        I now know,
gentle feelings
        perchance to grow.
Perchance, in covert
        love to seek-
What my words here
        have sought to speak.

I'll give you this promise
to hold you for me:
When all of this passes
and our thoughts are free,
I'll ask you to near
and share a new life
and if you are happy
to become my wife.
I have always loved you
as lover and friend.
Nothing that now passes
could put that at end.
I will cherish and keep you
with laughter and play.
I will lie warm beside you
at birth of each day.
I'll touch you in passion
and soothe all your tears
and bring you the peace
you've sought through the years.
Know as you read this,
and when far away,
You've never been loved
more than you are today.

When you are near
      and warm to touch,
I feel our past
      and long so much
that in our shadows,
      so deep and cold,
we had each other's,
      arms to hold;
That fires born
      of memories past
could lead us to
      a way to last.
To capture new
      what we had then,
to feel again
      our where and when.
That on our parting,
      sorrowed ways,
the sun might rise
      on brighter days.
Be at dawn
      we, one, or two,
remember still
      my love for you.

I remember your breast,
the curve of your thigh,
the moments of pleasure
when sometimes you cry,
the taste of your hair
so wet on my lips,
the smooth of you skin,
the push of your hips,
the arch of your back,
the warmth of your hand,
the gentle caresses
on places not tanned.
When laying together
in life's true embrace,
there's nothing around us
we cannot erase.
Over your body only,
my fingers must roam,
for you are my life,
your bed is my home.

Tomorrow you'll miss me
    to face day alone,
asking in new ways
    what has to be known.
Seeking some pathway
    through life's troubled storm.
Is love growing cold
    or will be warm?
I can but advise you,
    with counsel and care,
that what we see now
    we can nurture and share
I love you so deeply
    I want only you
I need to be with you
    if you need it too.

Angel of my morning,
        how I miss your smile,
the sparkle of your eyes,
        that lingers for the while,
The fragrance of your laughter
        that brings my day to light,
the softness of your touching
        in the shadows of the night.
You give me love I don't deserve
        but this I tell you true,
You'll never know a greater love
        than yet I'll give to you.

40th Anniversary

Gather we this night to measure
forty years of friends we treasure,
with our praise and joyous cheers
to mark the passage of those years
How quickly memories pass us by
as moments into years must fly.
The child of yesterday is grown;
The home we bought, we finally own;
The dreams we had, have come to be;
The twig we planted, now a tree
The night proclaims that love can last
to build as two, a fruitful past.
These simple words can't truly say
all that's needed on this day.
But as you start on forty-one,
we know you've only just begun.
From our hearts, this gentle song,
<u>Live in love and prosper long</u>.

<u>Tami</u>

I want you to know,
        with blond hair and all,
with sparkling blue eyes
        and standing so tall,
that your father loves you
        like no one before,
and no one to come
        will love you more.
You are my first child;
        you're made of my stuff,
and I'm here to help
        when things get too rough.
The thing about daughters--
        they are smarter than Dad.
They've got part of Mommy
        that I never had.
That makes you so special,
        the best of us two.
You can do anything
        if you really want to.
So hold your head high,
        be the best in the crowd.
Sometimes I could cry,
        because I'm so proud.

Rescue

I lie on my bunk
    in the stillness of night
with sleep on my left
    and thoughts on my right.
On the window above
    leaves scratch the pane
and shadows are dancing
    in tune with the rain.
I sense in the darkness
    a call will come in
to shatter the quiet
    as sirens begin.
Sheets take to flying,
    the floor start to shake,
The lights and the doors
    will quickly awake.
The clanging of helmets,
    few words are said,
the first engine fires,
    the first flashing red...
In a moment it's over,
    only blankets remain
where minutes before
    the sleepers had lain.
I know as I doze
    to await the alarm,
someone is safer
    and farther from harm.
A smile warms my heart
    as eyes start to close,
of all of God's children
    it's us that He chose
to join here as friends
    in silence to lie
'til someone's in need-
    to answer their cry.

Often I am searching
          for a thought or word,
whether to approach you,
          wether to be heard.
I know you'll always love me
          and answer a request
But do you ever need me?
          Should I let it rest?
Should I wait for trouble
          to bring your tearful call?
Should I only be there
          to catch you when you fall?
Do you need to hear me
          in just a simple way?
Is it better weekly
          than every other day?
You need my greater friendship
          than ever need my touch
How am I to reconcile
          loving you too much?

My wife's in love –
      a funny phrase;
it tickles her
      throughout her days.
It brings such joy
      and fancy free,
such radiant eyes
      and schoolgirl glee.
She sees the morn
      a different way.
A different song
      her soul delay.
In leaps and bounds
      her heart apace,
To meet the eyes,
      her lovers's face,
to hear his voice,
      her fear to still,
To learn and grow,
      her life fulfill.
On wings of love
      to soar anew
through sunlit skies
      of aqua blue.
To spin around,
      as if new sight,
had brushed away
      the clouds of flight.
So beautiful,
      this touch of life,
this newfound love
      that holds my wife.

Friends are such rare things,
      like diamonds and wine,
with value and luster
      increasing with time.
If not for such treasures,
      to have and to hold,
what purpose in living,
      except to get old?

I feel like I should be with you every minute
    but I should give you space.
I feel like I should turn you loose to grow
    but I don't want to miss it.
I feel like I should cling to you
    but I should let someone else.
I feel like being your friend
    but like a lover,
I feel like I'm watching a beloved pet
    turned loose in the wild to be free.
I feel somewhat at a loss with myself,
    and with you.

I know not how to speak to you.
    I know not where or why.
I cannot seem to touch your cheek
    or kiss you when you cry.
You're halfway mine and then gone again,
    a moment's passing pause,
like a stream of treasured trout
    slipped through grizzlies' claws.
I know not how to fade away
    but only stay, and smile,
hoping that on the carousel's
    next spin, you'll stop awhile.

You know you'll never be happy with me
      so where are we going?
You want me to be there and hold you,
      just to be safe,
but you don't want me to need you,
      or take from you much.
You want me to be only what you want
      and not what I am.
When I'm not, I might as well be alone
      for you're not happy.
You know I'll never please you;
      why do you want me to try?

There's really something lost here,
but is it her or me,
enveloped in a deepened fog
as far as I can see?
I think it may be just a while
before it comes to nest,
but could be that the light is out,
forever, dark, at rest.
The loneliness absorbs me,
as I wrestle with my fate
will I ever find you, love?
or is it soon too late?

The edge is not so far now
        the drop is not so deep
the abyss is much dearer
        than promises to keep
I want to feel the falling,
        the easing of my heart,
the sleepy, peaceful void of life
        awaits, if I could start
It is much closer, sweeter
        so beckoning a song
the fatal lonely solitude
        for which I dearly long.

You are growing beyond me
in ways unforeseen,
with smiles and with laughter
and love in between,
to lands of new promise,
to things ever sought
to skip through life's gauntlet
and never be caught.
But where you are going,
I cannot be along.
I don't know the words
and can't hear the song.
You are well to becoming
what you always could be.
I love you too dearly
to not set you free.

My wife thinks she's pregnant-
now that's quite a twist!
It's certainly more trouble
than she ever wished!
With dark hair and dark eyes
from a husband who's fixed,
to explain its appearance
is some bag of tricks.
But why does this shadow
cloud over her today?
The fate of the rabbit
is six weeks away.
She cries of the loss
of virginity's glow,
that the pedestal fell
and left her so low.
The beautiful Princess
held by worry's fear
needs more than ever
to be free and clear.
She's burning her bridges
before they are built-
That the love all around her
will wither and wilt.
I cling to her softly,
for I love her still,
and ease through her nightmares,
for I always will.
My wife thinks she's fertile
from some other's seed,
but I know she's not
and I'm all that she'll need.
For we are forever!
Neither worry nor doubt
can alter love's flame
or smother it out.

I will always love you
together or apart.
You hold a magic moment
in the corner of my heart.
I will always need you
to make me laugh and smile.
You have a charm to keep me
lingering a while.
I will always want you
as a lover and a friend.
You have the touch of passion
that never wants to end.
I will always love your
silliness and all.
I will always answer
when you need to call.

Torn between two lovers
        like going through a sieve.
You'd like to be the taker
        but seems you always give.
Just when you should be soaring,
        the breezes all turn still,
spinning, tumbling in your mind
        can cause your heart a spill.
There is no easy pathway
        to split your love in two.
Laughing smiles and tears of hurt
        belong to all of you.
At some point there will be just one
        and then where will you be –
Sailing high or undertowed
        by the ever constant sea?

Yesterday was happiness;
    today is underground.
Oh, how joyful life would be
    if only fate were round.
Love, how things are changing,
    turning us away,
from what we thought so special
    only yesterday.

Your fingertips slide softly
        off my outstretched palm,
next to me your body cold
        belies the gentle calm.
Missing is the fire
        that used to grace your eyes,
buried is the passion
        that used to bring love's sighs.
In the early morning,
        I watch your subtle form
searching for a window
        into where our hearts were warm.
I cannot touch the feelings
        that made us into one
I cannot find the answer
        for why it came undone.
But lying in the sunlight
        as shadows streak your hair,
I know that you are somewhere else
        and wish that I was there.
Through my tears on leaving,
        your body seems to glow.
The fire in my breaking heart
        burns more than you can know.
I would not trade our moments
        even knowing what they cost;
they will keep me in the game
        that I've already lost.

Hope that springs eternal,
        from hearts so far away,
that time may find an opening
        for two as one someday.
Every passing moment
        that fate allows us share,
brings a deeper knowingness
        and fosters love and care.
Content within your loving,
        peaceful as your friend,
I can live forever
        knowing we won't end.
But if there is a time for us,
        when moments become years,
It's nice to know, my angel,
        hope lingers in your tears.
Dreams are made of fragileness,
        like crystal flakes of snow,
weaving us together
        in a love just we can know.

If you're ever loving,
      and don't what him to stop,
keep your KY handy
      and place yourself on top.
Move with all devotion,
      a gentle swirling drive;
squeeze him with your passion
      to keep his manhood live.
Liven up the tempo,
      from your throat recall
the words and sighs to softly
      take him up the wall.
Then when the moments over,
      and spilled across the sheet
let him know that he's the best;
      no one could compete.

She blossoms with a fire
        that men cannot resist,
but when I see her dance card,
        my name's off the list.
She gives with all her spirit;
        her passion rises high.
But lost within the years and tears,
        it passes me right by.
What is gone is precious;
        it hurts to recognize
that when her smile is happy,
        it's someone else's eyes.
She blossoms with a fire
        I wish that I could start,
for in her eyes is everything
        that burns within my heart.

I miss you as I sit here,
        the quiet creeping past,
the moments once to share you,
        the gentle feelings last.
What hours we have cherished
        in all these twenty years
seem but a pond's reflection
        of a distant lover's tears.
The ripples fan out wider
        and catch the April breeze,
painted by the sunbeams
        swaying in the trees.
Hand in hand we strolled then
        through the fields and streams,
retracing magic footfalls,
        alive in memories' dreams.
For in this silent interlude
        we share from far apart,
love is peaceful waiting
        in the corner of my heart.

You must find more patience
    to give life a chance,
to live out your dreams
    and hopes for romance.
A marriage is something
    that flows with the wind
in many directions,
    though not toward an end.
The growth can be painful
    but not smile through the tears.
the day to day turmoil
    will soften o'er years.
For always tomorrow
    is unknown and new,
with unseen horizons
    between you and me.
Smile in the sunlight;
    Dance in your heart.
There's nothing about us
    that says we will part.
You first must recover
    from your thunderstorm.
The cold that you feel
    is really lukewarm.
Things we have lost
    through times not withstood,
could open new ways
    for times to be good.
The ocean still calls us
    and bids us as two.
The poet still writes
    love words for you.
Can we survive this?
    Beyond friendship and care?
What do we want?
    So here is the dare:
I dare you to quit
    as weak as you seem,
for I still do love you
    as much as you dream.

You must let me find mine
      and balance my life.
First be my princess,
      then be my wife.

I hurt for you
        this summer day,
are you are hurting
        so far away.
I wish for you
        a peace of mind
like that which we
        together find.
I know your falling
        tears in pain
because around me
        splashes rain.
And with the storm,
        the crashing sea
drifts your broken
        heart to me.
Though I can't help
        the pieces heal,
with all my love
        I care, I feel.

I cannot see for the fog
        slowly surrounding
                turning as I
                        turn

How long have I turned?
        how slowly?
                how lost?

I can see my hand
        but not touch
                or feel.

20th HS Reunion

The tear in my eye
      from 20 years past,
a remembrance of you
      and lots that were cast,
the salt of the memory
      of love of our youth,
not nurtured with age
      but still living in truth.
How I did love you!
      Old feeling arise:
the wet of your lips,
      the smile in your eyes.
If only the magic
      maturing can teach
of loving and sharing
      was then in my reach.
To capture a moment,
      so long overdue
to caress a soft blossom
      like the touch of the dew.
To sing you a ring
      of the gentlest chime,
to love you forever,
      if just for a time,
but for the tear
      and its lonely streak,
I must let it be
      and not memories seek.
For you and your life,
      now 20 years through,
don't even imagine
      what makes my heart blue.
I can but hope
      if our meeting takes place,
the love in my soul
      you can read in my face,
and then for an instant,
      a short timeless gaze,

you'll know that I've loved you
for all of these days.

Shadows

From yesterdays
    soft thoughts arise
beneath the tranquil,
    summer skies.

Two past shadows
    form at night
again, by chance,
    their hearts alight.

O'er flowing time.
    a gentle breeze
restores a share
    of memories.

Dreams and stars,
    for just a while –
the shadows touch,
    and laugh, and smile.

Park Rangers

Sleeping, I wandered
through the woods of my mind,
stumbling through briars
when what did I find:
but a cute little ranger
and old Smokey the Bear,
romping and playing
with hardly a care.
"See, I've come ready
for 9 weeks," she said,
"come play with my fire
on a pine needle bed."
Now this seemed quite odd,
as well you might ask,
but being a bear he
went straight to the task.
So out of this dream,
that formed in my brain,
the image was clear
of how park rangers train.

Shadows and night lights
        play on the sill.
The mood in the air
        is quiet and still,
except for the secret
        whispers and sighs.
The glow of your face
        from love in my eyes
wraps us in love
        that we deeply share.
Holding you gently,
        caressing your hair,
lost in the passion
        of caring so much,
melting, as softly,
        as lips come to touch.
Feel in my arms,
        know in your heart,
saying 'I love you'
        is only a start.

To feel love again,
    after years and tears,
    after thunder and lightning,
        and streams of fallen rain
            on roofs and gutters and
                downspouts and curbs
                    and sewers
        in puddles and splashes,
            in mist and fog,
  is like rebirth.

The emerging rainbow
    from cloudy sky,
        of steam and humidity,
        of songs of birds
            ruffled and fluttering,
        of blossoms new
            and simmering grass,
        of glistening drops
            of sunlight,
  and life.

The butterfly
    silently, fickly alighting,
        and aloft,
        and free.

To feel love again--
    to touch gently
      to soar,
        to fly reckless and wild,
        tethered only
          by you
            and your smile,
              and the rest of our lives.

Where is the fire
      we kindled and made,
the flames of our passion
      where we once played?
Am I to lose you
      to cold wind and rains
that try to torment us
      from outside the panes?
Your touch is now short,
      but silences long;
Have you abandoned
      our beautiful song?
Tomorrows are hard
      to find and to hold.
How do I keep you
      until we grow old?

<u>Daughters</u>

I have watched you
      all of these years,
from learning to walk
      to love's first soft tears,
through snowflakes and thunder,
      in joy and in pain,
from dancing in sunlight,
      to drenching in rain.
You fill me with wonder,
      as memories delay,
from years of your growing
      to blossom today.
And I will keep watching,
      from near or afar,
for the love of your father
      is tied to your star.

Rose

Soft rays of morning
      mix with your curls
           and flow o'er your shoulders
                  in streaks and in swirls,

glowing, it warms
      the hue of your skin
           enwrapping the beauty
                  that lies deep within.

In stillness, in peace,
      such gentle repose;
           dawn's precious kiss
                  envelops a rose.

What will we remember
    years from now
        about tonight-
            about love lost or gained?

Will you feel the firelight
    so distant?

Will your dreams foreshadow
    your heartbreak?

Will I remember the bittersweet
    of pain and promise
    of what you may leave
        and what you may keep?

Will you remember where the love really is
    so that
        years from now
            there will be us to remember?

Or will this fire be
    a memory
        rather than a torch?

What is it I'm missing
        at rest on the lawn?
                The breeze tickles my ear,
                        but not my fancy.
The grass quivers and waves
    but not to me-
    The gentle ripples moving away to river's edge
           to become ripplets and swirls
                    to caress some shore afar.

Sun's rays dance on my skin and my book
            at ease and with grace
                  and laughter floats in the air
            The sun's light streaks
                to warm everything
                      and everyone
                            but me.

A leaf from a tree's new life
        drifts softly along
                the ridges and tufts of wind
                      and lands on my hand,
                          in my thoughts.

The blossom is missing
        and so her touch.

I never thought
      I'd find you,
or love again
      so strongly.
I thought of
      moments blue,
nights of cold
      and lonely-
of Autumn
      coming fast,
and cloudy
      skies above,
so buried
      in the past,
so needing
      just to love.
Then with a
      winter sky,
with images
      and with tears,
a new love
      was begun,
and from one
      kiss endures.
Finding you
      so gently,
and knowing
      from the start,
I will wait
      so dearly,
Forever,
      for your heart.

This is the hardest
       love has been
              with still life to come
      It is at times unbearable
              and yet it's just begun.

In my words
       before this
              there has always been solace
Now there's just
       sore empty spots
              and feelings without place.

Will you ever
       push him out
              and will I fill your heart
      before I cannot
             linger more
                    and from your side depart?

Gently kissing in the sky,
        the leaves and branch intertwine,
dancing to a distant song
        as to the breeze incline.
Does not love so also bend
        and sway, as if to play
music for the heart to hear
        against the mind to lay.
Over years it changes such,
        each Spring its life anew,
that we can only marvel
        the depth and shape and hue.
Is not love also growing?
        that as two souls mature,
the years interweave them
        so through life endure.

Ripples

The vows we take across the years
    like morning ripples on a lake
expanding 'yond the laughs and tears
    would seem to end just out of sight
    but linger, as the still of night

Why then to give a solemn pledge
    like a rooting of a seed
if, with time, a change allege
    so foliage in its growing time
    when mature, is past its prime?

Perchance the secret gently lies
    like breezes 'round a willow
in contentment's peaceful sighs
    whether calm or whether gale
    uplifts love beyond its fail.

A rose in the springtime
    blossoms with gold,
        from the sun, token of love
            to the young and the old.
Love's beauty that lasts
    under the heat
        in the summer of life,
            over bitter and sweet.
Then in its autumn
    mature in soft ways,
        a bountiful harvest
            within shortened days
With those who are touched
    by its deep glow,
        love glistens bright
            like new-fallen snow.

```
The quiet one
     sits
          still
               in her bay window
                    waiting
                         for the snow
                              alone
Clouds darken
     the sky
          chilling like
               frost on the window
                    the edges
                         of heart strings.
Snowflakes swirl,
     the emptiness
          around
               and around
          like music and friendship
               growing
                    and hurting
Far beyond
     the winters of youth
          and storms
               and bitter cold
                    and stillness
A star awaits
     shining
          bringing the fire of hope
               watching
                    caring
                         loving forever,
the quiet one.
```

Promise on T Street

Twas the night before Sunday
    and all on T street,
the homeless were milling
    with nothing to eat,
the hookers and beggars
    were starting to roam,
with the music of sirens,
    I started this poem.
When into my thoughts
    there arose a short story,
about a young woman
    mid sadness and glory,
who always had Christmas
    with family at home,
but now faced the day
    very much on her own.
Who in the last year,
    of growing apart,
carried such burdens
    on so young a heart.
A story beginning
    with no virtual end,
that I'll never see
    or even pretend.
A tale like the stockings
    hung by the fire,
of promise and giving
    and fulfilling desire.
For after the darkness,
    that often portends,
follows the sunlight
    and soft morning winds.
For over the snow fields,
    through frostbitten air,
always is warmth
    when you dare and you care.
The wiseman of T street
    as he fades into night,
knows, like himself,
    she'll find her starlight.

Renovation

Muted strands of iodized light
filter through the tepid glass
and weary wood of the skylight,
casting a soft din over the bed,
slipping among the gentle shadows.
The cacophony beyond the old brick
only penetrating enough to be known,
but not disrupting isolation within.
The dust of decades past, and moments past,
settles, remains, touching every corner,
leaving no traces or stories behind.
The brilliant cobalt of the comforter and
the rich grain of the carpet it grazes
are but memories in the darkness,
stillness which bonds all as one.
In the oasis of night,
caught between promise and peace,
if sleep slips into the covers,
will I roll toward the wall or the unseen door?

I met my dearest, longest love
in the gentleness of May,
when youth and springtime flourish
and laughter fills the day.
when the burdens and the trappings
of life are freshly learned,
of love and song still intermixed,
of innocence unburned.
Sharing came so sweetly,
the breeze through bowing tree;
through the contact of her gaze,
I touched eternity.

Passion

Passion has its fragile side,
    apart from love's desire,
        as if in seeking to abide
            it withers from the fire.

Perhaps the richness of the fuel,
    is only surface deep;
        impurities begin to cool
            the core of loving's heat.

In the light of afterglow,
    with shadows intertwine,
        will the lovers find they know
            now, secrets not divine?

Arising from abed at morn
    to clothe the naked night
        the ecstasies so newly born
            burn harsher in the light.

This is a crossroads up ahead
    where drifts of snow converge
where tracks and trails left before
    form a new diverge.
I am beckoned to the left,
    as you must take the right;
for the first time in some years
    a separate Christmas night.
Once upon a Christmas Eve
    you let me share your bed,
and in the dawn your loving
    awoke my sleepy head.
I was filled with joy and peace
    all Christmas morning through;
While those several hours passed,
    our love was all I knew.
As now we face another time
    with changes in the wind,
deep within your lonely heart
    a loving wish I send.
A part of me will follow you
    and long to touch your face,
when early sun caresses you
    in a far and friendly place.
Love can't simply fly away
    as winter breezes blow-
I will always love you, Kate
    wherever you may go.

It's quiet now
    peaceful
        but empty without you.

Music fills my ears
    and soothes my thoughts,
        but not my longing.

Night skies have begun,
    dark, windy,
        bringing more than chills.

There is always dawn,
    I know,
        hope in warmth and light.

Missing you is hard,
    unhappy,
        but worth the wait.

Sometimes in my wondering,
      I come across a dream.
I come across a blossom
      reflected in a stream
that flows thru ageless forests,
      shaded by the trees,
gently soaking sunlight,
      laughing in the breeze.
I gaze up softly searching
      the song birds in the sky,
and lay on a grassy knoll
      let the day just pass me by.
At times to touch the thoughts
      that bring you ever near,
that sow my heart with gladness
      and sprinkle me with cheer,
that lift me from my wondering
      to dreams 'round every bend,
the glimpse of love that lingers,
      and hastens wondering's end.

25th Reunion

Something about you
    reminds me of then,
the crispness of Fall,
    the leaves in a spin,
pom-poms and bonfires,
    cheering and tears,
memory still cherished
    of earlier years.
Something about you
    has touched me again,
brought to the surface
    feelings of when
dancing was loving,
    flirting was art,
laughter was music
    from strings of the heart.
Something about you
    transcends the past,
lightens the shadows
    life's struggles cast.
A smile and a sparkle,
    a lingering kiss,
more than this evening,
    you I will miss.

This is a place of old loneliness
   where memories of past lives
         lie in the undisturbed dust
     blend into the dirty floors and dull plaster walls
       trapped and unchanging

There is a peace here
      where laughter once held court and tears flowed
        from dreamers and lovers
           lain on their beds
               upon a time ago

The silence here
      drapes over the railings and debris lingering
        with room for new brooding or moods
        as one would choose

There was us here
      the foundations set firmly and truly prepared
         to set life free again inside our joint walls
         now trapped and unchangeable

There is healing in this place
   where pain finds relief in the space and the shadows
    carved as crystals of the sun
      shatter against the ceiling
         carom off artifacts of you.

The sound of your voice is like music
    swirling around me
        lifting my spirit and dancing
            around in my solitude,
                so far away from you
I could listen for days
    to the melodies that ease me
        into gentler moods
            and hopeful dreams,
                so far away from you
You sew threads of joy
    through the people
        and the fabric
           which holds them,
                so very near to you
There is a radiance
    you sprinkle like sun dust
        that adheres just so
           and lingers long
                after touching you
I am warmed by the coals
    you gently kindled
        and now keep stoking
           until I'm again
                so very close to you.

Londontown

Fall has reached this peaceful shore,
but you'd never know it.
Leaves still green and sunny skies
touch me where I sit.
The gentle lapping of the waves
surrounds me on the pier.
The breezes lift and spin my hair
as I linger here.
Along these banks in other times,
ships would dock and load
the staples of Colonial life
as South River flowed.
Now in gentle solitude
the river passes by,
time and history glide along,
like clouds in the sky.
The spirits and the footsteps,
all that now reside,
lead my heart to ponder
life's unsteady tide.
Somehow in the wind and wave,
I suddenly am free
of all the history and the loads
burdensome to me.
Where it leads, I cannot know,
but with hope anew,
whatever future lies ahead,
I can share with you.
I know it's been too short a time,
since we met and danced,
for you to know the love in me
and find your heart entranced.
This I know: I want it all.
I see, in you, my life.
I want to touch forever
with you as my wife.
Someday I will bring you here,
when Fall has just begun,
so you may share the joyousness
with which my heart was won.

California

I heard what they said
of nuts and of flakes:
"It must be the Sun."
"It must be the grapes."
"Don't send your kids
to school in L.A.,
they'll be more normal
if you keep them away."
The smog, and the gangs,
the drugs and the hair;
the cops and the gays
all mingling there.
"One day an earthquake
will wash them asea;
and cleanup the coast -
just wait and see!"
What have you guys done
to get such bad press?
Did all the sex and
the surf cause the mess?
Surely you see the
errors of your ways.
Remember your Mom:
"Dear, crime never pays"
So come to the East,
where you can be free
of sin and live clean
in New York, or DC.
Where love is closed up
in our puritan past,
and youth is just something
one has to get past!

Fairy Tale

In this small moment,
    as night gathers in,
the streaks and the shadows
    where sunlight had been,
I lie in the quiet,
    when heartbeats are felt,
and ponder the deuces
    and aces life dealt.
Fragments of music,
    rain from the tears,
coals from the fires,
    rivers of fears,
mixtures and tinctures,
    distilled long ago,
swirl with the feelings
    that now gently flow.
Dancing with fairies,
    bright-eyed and gay,
easing the burdens
    required by day.
Lo, she appears
    in her shimmering gown
reaching to touch me
    as I'm kneeling down.
I become champion,
    fearless and bold.
She is my lover
    to have and to hold.
Then comes the daybreak,
    a new morning sun,
dragons to conquer,
    the castle to run.
But Excalibur's blade
    sings true to say:
Our eternal love
    transcends everyday.
Whatever the timing,
    or distance apart,
The Princess will thrive
    of the love in my heart.

Forever cannot be described;
    it only can be sensed,
like the wildest spirit
    neither is it fenced
by words or times or places,
    it merely has to grow.
Like a love that holds your heart,
    you simply have to know,
that after all tomorrows,
    through our lives so long,
You and I will harmonize
    one great and loving song.

Proposal

Will you grace my mornings
      with gentle falling rain-
misty, peaceful patterings
      upon my window pane?

Will you fill night's shadows
      with the splash of dawn,
trickling rays of sunbeams
      that dance across the lawn?

Will you warm my evenings
      and etch away the frost?
Will you light the fire
      that beckons when I'm lost?

Will your spirit dream with me
      and wish upon a star
that shines so bright with love
      and joy even from afar?

And will you give me promise
      that as I age and die,
you will stay beside me
      and hold me as I lie?

Will you be my partner
      and dear beloved wife?
Will you share my greatest love
      -for you, for all your life?

I'm forever seeing you
      on the backyard swing,
flying hair and sunlight,
      gentle laughter's ring.
Up so high you're flying,
      your petticoat and skirt,
trailing just behind you,
      skimming off the dirt,
then down again, a giant whoosh,
      and up the other way,
your eyes reflect the azure sky;
      your smile reflects the day.
I 'll be always keeping you,
      in this special place
and when I'm most in need of it,
      I'll recall your face.
For I will travel far and wide,
      perchance a fortune win,
but I will always linger
      on the swing with Carolyn.

The silence of the early morn,
    without the siren and the horn
that plague the night as I to bed,
    alas the days events to shed,
cradles me in soft peacefulness.
    I lie beneath the cover's mess
warming against the chilly air
    that also filters sunlight there,
as dawn slowly begins to grow.
    Once dark and shapeless curtains glow
as shadows swiftly dart away
    to corners hidden from the day.
Golden light like small fingers streaks
    among your hair, o'er your cheeks,
cascading off your nose and chin,
    pooling on your pearl-like skin.
Lying tangled around you, I
    can hear soft music in your sigh,
and magic flows within my veins
    as quickly now the nightfall wanes.
Your eyes alive, though full with sleep,
    touch me with a love so deep.
No more in waking could I want-
    these feelings that in me haunt
my days and fuel my heart's desire
    (and also kindle passion's fire).
I would speak, if words wouldn't fail
    my great love to you unveil.
There is no greater joy in life
    than early morning with my wife.

At times of great shadows
I stand midst the trees
and hear the great branches
swing free with the breeze.
I know that the seasons
have many times flown-
'fore even I was,
the forest was grown.
Its shade a great comfort,
its stillness such peace,
it lingers majestic
as if time to cease.
And in its tall spires
such stories to tell,
woven by silence,
with a soft magic spell.
It's easy to tarry
and cherish the morn,
to touch the old trunks
so ancient and worn.
But soon one less monarch
will christen the sky;
its limbs hanging loosely
portending to die.
The last turn of the leaves,
last nip of the Fall;
my friend and my solace
won't answer Spring's call.
New blossoms around it
may ease my dismay
that just when I'm closest,
it's taken away.

Gentle breezes great this day
        a peaceful melody,
lightly skipping, smile to smile
        in love's harmony.
Sharing in our company,
        the beauty of the bond--
A window to the happiness
        that leads, from now, beyond.

Kari Sweet Sixteen

My quiet one, you reach the age
    that once we labelled 'sweet'
A time gone by, of simpler days,
    a different drummer's beat.
My troubled one, the pressures bear
    upon your everyday;
Prayers and dreams beyond this time
    seem now, so far away.
I wish for you a peaceful growth-
    to learn of life, of song,
of joy, of dance, of play,
    of love that lingers long.
When I was but the age you are,
    girls could grab my heart,
and every time they wandered past,
    I felt the passion start.
The Beatles were the hottest group;
    The mini skirt was in;
Drugs were just prescriptions;
    Corvettes were Porsches then.
Records outsold tapes by far;
    We had no MTV;
Movies had no sex or blood;
    and 'average' grades were B.
But I remember how it felt,
    those many days ago,
to face uncertain days ahead
    with so much more to know.
I never got to know my Dad
    for he was rarely well,
and Mother never understood,
    what little I could tell.
So I looked to friends a lot,
    or spent my thoughts alone,
sometimes I was so desperate too--
    the worst I've ever known.
But even as I tell you this,
    I know you too will find
that all these trials and troubles
    will soon fall far behind.

At sixteen driving opened doors
      and true love left its touch;
College meant escaping home,
      and freedom meant so much.
I will always think of you
      as just my little girl,
of when you'd run to greet me,
      up in my lap you'd curl.
However, too, I see in you
      the woman soon to be-
A spirit to be proud of,
      just aching to be free.
On this day and those to come,
      wherever far you roam,
deep and safe within my heart,
      you'll always find a home.

Wedding Anniversary

Just around the corner
a man sits in his chair
warming by the fireplace
and in his eyes a stare
that lingers in the quiet
contentment in his heart
lounging in the dimness
as sparks and shadows dart.

Just around the corner
in her matching chair
sits a timeless beauty
firelight in her hair
resting under blanket
to stop the winter chill
silently her heartsong
fills the evening still.

Just around the corner
sleep and dreams abide
at the end of fire's light
when thoughts and eyes subside
Under cover, under cloth,
the gentle touch portends:
a union bound forever
of lovers and best friends.

I touched April yesterday
       and kissed
              the eyes of the sky.
I felt the wind of her love
       wrap around me
              and the warmth
                      of her smile awaken me.
I saw the sparkle
       of newly moistened fields
              and the blossoming
                      of dreams....
              the tenderness of down
                      stroked my cheek.
I tasted sweet Springtime
       with the purity
              of melting snow.
I heard the song
       of trees laughing
              in her breezes
                      gently brushing
                              her rain-caressed hair.
I stood lost in beauty
       and dazzled with life.
I reached to kiss the face of the morn
       and linger there
              from April's touch.

I opened an old file today
and photos tumbled free.
The first of many shots to come,
at the start of you and me.
Beneath the sunny LA sky,
we stand there, holding hands.
Just as we were finding out
our universe's plans.
You were bright and beautiful,
as you stay each year,
and I was wildly happy at
the joy of being near.
For though the time is passing,
and the photograph now old,
the love that burns for you in me,
still keeps the candle bold.

The words not ever spoken
are not like songs unsung,
for still a message lingers
though not a bell has rung.
The words not ever spoken
hide deep within a soul,
and drift at sea forever
'til washed up on a shoal.
The words not ever spoken
o'er time transform the land
from sweetly tranquil coastlines
to sadly littered sand.
The words not ever spoken
may seem to ease the pains,
but in those swallowed musings,
one loses more than gains.
The words not ever spoken
is not the way I live,
for thru my thoughts and feelings
is life I choose to give.
The words not ever spoken
are easier to take;
And, because I love you, it's
a choice I cannot make.

I wanted to write you
a poem at the top
of my form and, my love,
a verse without stop.
But it takes me some time,
these words to compose,
to precisely describe
a beautiful rose.
All through the day long
I tried to get free.
to trumpet the joy
of your company;
To speak of the peace
and love in my heart
that you as my wife
have come to impart.
the whispers of kids,
the moaning of lust,
the laughter to tears,
the deepness of trust.
Alas, the day ends
no nearer my aim,
and still you 'll await
this poem just the same.
So let me just say,
that words aren't enough
to tell you I love you
and all of that stuff.

Drifting along on dark, swelling seas,
      I watch as your boat passes by.
The mist in your eye, and of the surf,
      match the gray doom of the sky.
Where do you journey, my lady so fair,
      as the currents drag you along?
What do you seek as waves bounce around?
      What storm has so silenced your song?
I 've a taut line to toss from ashore
      to haul your small craft to the beach.
But in your gaze no trace of desire,
      a lingering just out of reach.
Is there not something seen in this storm,
      to brighten and lighten your way?
Must you asea in the cold overcast,
      and wander so far, far away?
I've built you this fire, deep in my heart,
      to guide you to warmth and to home.
I, and my love, will stay here and wait
      for however long you must roam.

For Billy Cochran

What seems a fleeting moment,
    a time and space too small,
has past us by too quickly
    and left an anguished call.
A journey of adventure.
    of mischief and of smiles,
A life with endless promise
    cut short by miles and miles.
Can we but remember,
    encircled now by friends,
all the joy and laughter
    'round that journey's bends.
Each one of us now honors,
    and celebrates inside.
that love and jubilation
    he left before he died.
And in those thoughts and feelings,
    remembrances we share,
whenever we revive them,
    he is always there.
In that – this piece of solace,
    that every memory gives:
that in our hearts of loving,
    He forever lives.

Father's Day

I look to you for words of trust,
through growing years,
and settling dust.

I glean from you life's subtleties,
from thunderstorms,
to gentle breeze.

I sing my trials to your ears,
to boost my soul
and ease my fears.

I bring my broken heart around
for silent hugs
and tears abound.

I share each joy and victory
wanting praise,
to bolster me.

I need your eyes to gently say
the soothing, caring
"It's ok".

I will always look to you
with deepened love
for all you do.

And Father, in my special way,
I celebrate
your life today.

Hazy, ain't it. Hot, humid tending to lazy.
    Skin baking, oozing,
        absorbing
  while errands and projects wilt
    and that laid-back, Southern drawl
      and lifestyle sneaks in
        where the day's ambition used to be.
Remember that old movie?
    The hefty, good-old-boy in his
      sweat soaked Sheriff uniform
        fanning his tenderized face
          with that broad, dusty hat with the badge,
  stepping out of the sun and through the door
      The ceiling fan noiselessly
          stirring the shadows on the floor
            in it's rhythmic way.
  the drops rolling down his broad neck,
    and down the neck of
        That ice cold Coca Cola,
  the "woo-wee" sliding from his lips,
    The big, rough back-of the-hand to the brow,
      the handkerchief to the back of the neck,
      the red, puffy eyes invariably drawn
        to the soft, summer dress
          clung to the breast
            of a local married woman,
          who happens to be there.
Did you ever want to be there,
    lost in that hazy, lazy time,
      nothing pressing.
      nowhere calling
        except that ice cold Coca Cola.

The Colonel's Birthday

Even old warriors have birthdays and age,
losing some memories but gaining as Sage.
The mighty, tall oak revered among trees,
sturdy and steady, unbent in the breeze.

Even old fathers have birthdays and age;
children now grown, less time to engage.
Keeper of knowledge, guide to the fun,
loved and respected by daughter and son.

Even grandfathers have birthdays and age,
reading to grandkids, turning each page.
Teller of stories, teacher, and friend;
wiper of tears when hearts are a-mend.

Even old husbands have birthdays and age,
more making projects than earning a wage.
At peace with his home, in love with his wife,
enjoying the rhythm of each day of life.

Even old friends have birthdays and age;
dearer and fewer they seem at this stage.
Cheering him on, singing his praise,
King of the nighttime, Lord of his days!

Even old warriors have birthdays and age
while serving in roles too numerous to gauge.
The hero, the leader, the trusted and true,
for pasts and for futures, we honor you.

South

Travelers we, easing home,
    find the side trip and side roads,
        renewing.
Driving up, up the mountain
    it looms high and graceful.

Yet the roadway twists and aches around curves,
    like the walk of the old gentle man
        sauntering, slowly on the gravel.
    like the turns of the parched stone wall
        that rises from the underbrush
        to keep us from the edge,
            from straying too far from the road
            as we pass.

Above us, surrounding us,
    the oak, the cypress, the willow,
        dripping moss
            on fern and briar, entangling roots
                and turning the hills into mystery
                and timelessness;

So high the branches dance as to blend the sky
    green on blue,
        blue on green
            as the breezes, twirling the leaves,
                give momentary hope
                    to escape the heat,
                        or just the humid haze.
Up we rise.

Around a bend, shade bathes us
    a sheltering calm,
        an alcove, a pause in our journey
            to meet an old friend
                in a place new to us.

Tall, and long
    the preserved dwelling fills the

                    space well between the earth
                            and the shade.
The old staircase winds its way to the side,
            up, twist, up,
                    to a front door on the 2nd floor.

She greets us framed in her ancient doorway,
            with that gentleness of Southern charm
                    that some are just born with,
            with that purity of heart
                    in the calmness of her smile,
            with that ever brightened candle burning
                    in the sparkle of her eyes.

A vision for a single moment,
            like a dewdrop suspended from a leaf,
                on this high mountain top
                    near the skies of Dixie,
                        enveloped in the peaceful, sylvan ways
                            of Antebellum forests.

There's something tall about her.

She stands well,
            like the comfort of great tradition
                    graceful,
                        elegant,
                            as beautiful as love's promise.

If I close my eyes softly,
    when a break in the pace
gives me the moment
    for internal space,
I can feel you beside me,
    legs draped on mine;
escaped to our world-
    in a snippet of time.
Quiet and dream-like,
    bonded and still,
loving the touches
    as we always will.

Safe, we were
	scant moments ago.
Sheltered in glass and metal
	and coolly, conditioned air
		in quiet, tinted shade.
Now deep in sharp-edged grass,
	blades strong in constancy of humidity
		and poised in the heat like stakes
			sharpened
				in defense of intruders.
Carcasses surround us
	half-eaten remains
		of recent, overripe fruit
			bleeds its juice
				decaying,
					while cooking in the withering sun.
The unseen buzz at us,
	chaotic attacks
		attracted to the sweat
			that rolls down our necks
				that sticks to us as we struggle.
A symphony of nature abounds,
	chirping,
	calling,
	Buzzing,
		announcing us, perhaps
			on our trek
				through this Southern jungle.
Finally,
	with a last labored breath,
		we arrive
			at the sanctuary
				of the concrete front porch.
Thankful,
	ever so glad,
		to have made it
			through my brother's front yard.

Seasons (for Holly Cratty)

Quiet, my dear friend,
    greeting me so gently
        with the wonder of snowfall
            swirling, floating,
painting the gray sky in glorious silence.
    Streaks of silver and white
        brushstrokes in the air,
dropping a soft coverlet over hidden grass,
    over the paths of many feet,
        weaving a single color quilt.
From this old porch, sheltered and dry,
    the elegant dance fills the eyes,
        with timeliness....
Trees bow, majestically, in cold embrace
    of ice and wind--
        Winter's lovely prayer.
A single snowflake, etched by God's hand,
    lazily somersaults, down to the pond,
        forming a frozen blanket.

Dawn, my joyous friend,
    fill my early rise
        with the promise of new life,
            awakening...
First sun invading the shadows,
    igniting the colors
        hidden by night,
rousing the pines to stretch,
    the grass to turn emerald,
        the squirrels to yawn.
From this porch, my coffee in hand,
    the Spring day begins
        in sweet harmony.
The songs of wrens and robins and jays
    carry on the breeze
        with insects' buzz.
A single drop of dew, collected during darkness,
    lingers on a blade of grass,
        then falls unheard to the lawn.

Rain, my longtime friend,
      come anew at day's end
            to melt Summer's heat,
                  thundering.....
drowning the grass, the flowers,
      pounding the shingles,
            turning dust to mud in a flash,
whipping the tree boughs,
      lighting the sky with fire
            reflected in my eyes.
This old porch offers no refuge;
      sheets of watery fabric,
            wrap around,
unforgiving, as torrents
      lash like a dragon's tail
            at all who venture forth.
A single drop bounces on my hand,
      dives to the ground,
            and builds a river.

Wind, my dear friend,
      whispering gently through tussled hair,
            streaking my cheek,
                  caressing...
Playing the white pine limbs against each other,
      a whispering song,
            a peaceful harmony of trees bending,
carrying the playful sounding waterfall,
      splashing oft and o'er the worn rock faces,
           rippling the pond below.
From this old porch, the symphony
   fills the edge of autumn
      with an ageless wonder:-
         A kaleidoscope of notes caught in the breeze.
Bushes rustle; the porch screen hums;
   oaks and birches and maples and juniper all bow,
            in swirls and twirls, dancing...
A single leaf, burnished by the seasons change,
     Soars, drifts, floats, touches the pond,
          exploding its colors in reflection.

Love, my greatest companion,
    come touch my passion
        and stir my deepest soul,
            again..
Rekindle the never forgotten
    dear memories and promise,
        of sweet longing,
of children and lovers laughing,
    of dancing too close,
        of moonlight and song.
This old porch, lit only by stars and moon,
    a peaceful sanctuary,
        perchance stop time.
To stand in the night,
    Through all seasons and changes,
        pondering, smiling...
A single firefly winks in the dark sky,
    darting, flirting, soaring
        like love's first kiss.

Birthday Wish

If I were the breeze,

I would sweep around you,
    caressing your cheeks
        and dancing in your hair.

If I were the breeze,

I would paint your face with sunlight
  with the gentleness of soft rain
    with the beauty of a butterfly
      touching down.

If I were the breeze,

I would surround you with things of wonder
    and great love.

For your birthday,
    I wish you the breeze.

Independence

I once stood in Concord,
where first blood was shed,
where monuments and statues
tell us of the dead.
I felt the strangest feeling,
standing on the grass,
that time reversed and took me
back to days gone past.
The ordinary simpleness
of working on the farm,
far removed from tyranny,
far removed from harm.
Though the docks of Boston
are many horse-days hence,
here was first our freedom's song,
behind each rock and fence.

I once stood in ignorance,
where patience grew but thin
shipwrecked dreams all twas left
to tell me where I'd been.
I felt the greatest longing,
an aching in my soul,
like life was simply waiting
for me to pay the toll.
The simpleness of letting go
brought the Truth so clear:
instead of chasing shadows,
light was ever near.
Though my path be crooked,
and miles out of the way,
in my heart is freedom's song,
this independence day.

Emma's 13th Birthday

I knew a girl who once lived here
    with Mom & Dad & John.
She sang and danced round the rooms
    and frolicked on the lawn.
Now she's grown beyond some things,
    now its boys not toys.
Soon to be a woman she,
    with all her guile and ploys..
Still she laughs and twirls her hair
    as if she's just a child,
And entering her 14th year,
    just as bold and wild.
How lucky we to have this gift
    of beauty, talent rare,
To celebrate this day of birth
    with the Princess fair.
Teenage years 'oft bittersweet;
    but she will find the way,
Knowing she is loved much more
    than simple words can say.

Like bedsheets hung on the line that flap in the wind,
    the rain flows in sheets shimmering.
A time when everything stops
    except the beating of drops against windowpane.
My mind remembers an early storm,
    the thunder booming in my soul,
        and the lightning etching my soul.
When the light was lost and dark sky filled my world,
    the joy of sunlight blotted out,
        sadness filling the corners of my thoughts.
I think of that storm at times.
    It floods back over me;
        It leads me to memories
Of love
    Of you
        Before....
Each time it rains now,
    A small tear glistens my eye,
        and I feel the loss of us together.
But rain is too, the renewal of things, of
    what gives life its nourishment
        and in that is hope
the unquenchable depth of cherishing you,
    The knowingness of forever bonding,
        The beauty of unparalleled love,
            The greatest gift, of serenity.

Two great spirits in lustful play,
perchanced to kiss one winter day,
knowing not that with that touch,
they would grow to love so much

Finding in each other true,
one kindred heart instead of two,
finding in each other's eyes
eternal love which came to rise.

Laughing, crying, holding tight,
through so many day and night,
their bond now grown ever strong
and life's become a happy song.

Moon beam nights and stars above,
special times to kiss and love,
dreams and plans of future life,
wedded now as man and wife.

If I could but touch you
for one magic flight-
through a day of surprises
and loving at night

If I could but feel you,
and lie for awhile,
with talk and with laughter
and many a smile.

If I could but see you
and gaze in your eyes,
we'd dance on moonbeams
below starry skies.

If I could but kiss you
and feel your lips part,
then you would know
the depth of my heart.

If I could but tell you
in words of a poem
how deeply I'll love you
and with you, I'm home.

Daybreak

Lost in the feeling.
    drifting away,
        warmed as the sun
            starts a new day.

Lost in my arms,
    drifting asleep;
        snuggling close,
            loving so deep.

Lost in the ocean
    of eternal bliss,
        sharing so sweetly
            first morning's kiss.

The sound of your voice is like music
    swirling around me,
        lifting my spirit and dancing
            around in my solitude,
                so far away from you
I could listen for days
    to the melodies that ease me
        into gentler moods,
            and hopeful dreams,
                so far away from you
You sew threads of joy
    through the people
        and the fabric
           which holds them,
                so very near to you
There is a radiance
    you sprinkle like sundust
        that adheres just so,
           and lingers long
                after touching you
I am warmed by the coals
    you gently kindled,
        and now keep stoking,
           until I'm again,
                so very close to you.

There's a song in my heart
that's with me each day.
It lingers more strongly
than words I can say.
I want so to touch it,
in sweet harmony,
to dance and to laugh
with what I can't see.
For now, I just smile,
longing to sing.
Who knows what music
tomorrow will bring?

Sitting beside you,
    feeling the breeze
whisper so gently,
    kissing the trees.
Looking upon you -
    soft, flowing hair;
deep, loving eyes -
    pulling me there
Here in the quiet,
    the moment serene,
love that is ours
    couldn't be foreseen.
Whether we ever
    touch in the night,
Closeness we share
    will always feel right.
Whatever the future,
    I'll not forget
times we have shared;
    how we first met.
Make love with me darling
    with passion and heart,
Bonded forever,
    even apart.

I feel you at lakeside
      on a crisp winter day,
strolling in silence,
      the poodles at play
beside you. Like breezes that
      swirl through your hair,
my arms are around you
      as if I were there.
Through cold is the air
      with snow on its way,
in the warmth of my love,
      forever you'll stay.
So many are the miles,
      apart is our life.
But in short stolen moments,
      you are always my wife.

Ghost

She hangs as if perched
as light as the air,
aglow in the dark
as she watches me there.
Keeping my silence,
soothing my night,
chasing the shadows
'til morning's first light.
If I reach out to touch,
she flitters away.
Who knows what she does
alone everyday.
But at dark she is there,
as I nod off to sleep,
my guide through the dreams
that crawl and that creep
forged in the mind,
tempered by heart,
until a new day
announces its start.
My guardian spirit
who found me of late,
are you still smiling,
as you patiently wait?
Will you protect me
o'er miles and o'er years;
are you the calm over
storms of my fears?
and sweet little ghost
lingered above,
are you the signal
of newly found love?

With life flowing on,
a song in my heart
keeps me close by,
when'er we're apart.
For when truly found,
love's never lost,
even when distance
seems like a frost.
Just a few moments
together again
and passion gets hot
as it's ever been.
Someday will bring us
closer, I know.
All that we've planted
will freely grow.
Dancing in sunlight,
cuddling at night,
The smiles and the laughter
we'll shine ever bright.

An ever-so-slight breeze takes hold of the steam
   rising from the coffee,
       swirling it in slow motion,
           then lifting it away into infinity.
She holds the cup pensively;
   Peacefulness radiates off her gently featured face,
        gazing into nowhere particular.
The moist air dries as morning grows,
   leaving the scent of the heat to come later.
Legs crossed in faded, familiar jeans,
   back against the comfort of an old chair,
       she fits the porch like an old Florida home
          bonds to the land.
Whatever chaos lingers from the past,
       whatever turmoil wrestles with her thoughts,
      they are quietly dispelled,
          by her soft, simple smile.

www.ingramcontent.com/pod-product-compliance
Lightning Source LLC
Chambersburg PA
CBHW031348040426
42444CB00005B/231